Giggles Galore

Jokes, Riddles, and Fun Facts
for Kids of All Ages

By Carole P. Roman

Illustrated by Leen Roslan

Disclaimer

This is a work of fiction. Names, characters, business, events, locations and incidents are the products of the author's imagination. Any resemblance to actual persons, living or dead, or actual events is purely coincidental.

978-1-950080-03-8 Paperback

Chelshire, Inc.

"Laughter is an instant vacation." Milton Berle

For my dad who found the humor in everything.
Dus is allas.

Giggles Galore

What is a joke?

Jokes come in all different styles but are created to do the same job. They make us laugh. Jokes can change a frown into a smile. A good chuckle can lighten a dreary day or even make us feel better.

Jokes have been around for hundreds of years. Some of them might not be as funny as they once were, but others can set off the giggles no matter how old they are. Here is a collection of jokes, some new and some so old your grandparents might recognize them.

So, open the book and find a joke that works for you.

Tell one and watch what happens.

Let the good times roll!

Food
Jokes

What do you call a sad strawberry?
A blueberry.

What resembles half a peach?
The other half.

Why do watermelons have fancy weddings?
Because they cantaloupe.

How do you make an apple turnover?

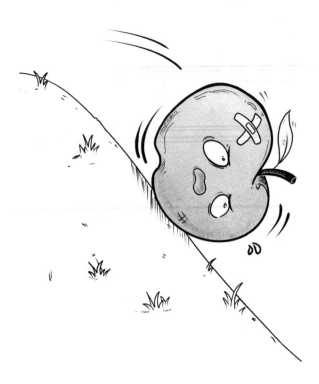

Push it downhill.

True or false
Johnny Appleseed was not a real person.

False - Johnny Appleseed's real name was John Chapman. He lived from 1774-1845 and was known as a kind and generous man. He became famous for planting apple trees in Pennsylvania, Ontario, Ohio, Indiana, and Illinois.

He walked barefoot and wore a tin pot for a hat.

People think he created orchards in vacant fields, but Appleseed planted well-thought-out nurseries to grow plentiful harvests for the farmers that lived in the area.

His apples were not good for eating. They were called 'spitters' because they were small and tart.

People would take a bite of these apples and spit it out!

They were used for apple cider. Water could harbor bacteria and be dangerous to drink, so apple cider was considered a safer alternative for drinking.

Johnny Appleseed loved nature and was considered a great conservationist.

In Nova, Ohio, you can visit one of the original trees planted by Johnny. It is 176 years old!

So, next time you eat an apple think of Johnny Appleseed and his mission to bring apples to every household.

Now that's a *Delicious* story!
(Delicious is the name of a tasty apple.)

Why didn't the banana sing to the dog?
Bananas can't talk.

How did the banana wear its hair?
In bunches.

What kind of monkey doesn't eat bananas?
An *orangutan*.

Why do oranges wear suntan lotion?
Because they peel.

What does an orange do when it takes a test?
Concentrates.

What do you call a group of
people dressed as asparagus?
Asparaguys.

Did you hear about the carrot detective?
He got to the root of the case.

What is red and goes up and down?
A tomato in an elevator.

True or false
Tomato is a fruit.

True - The tomato is the fruit of the tomato plant. Tomatoes are grown from the seeds of flowering plants, and is classified as a fruit.

They were first grown in the Andes, in South America, near Peru. There are more than 7500 different varieties of tomatoes.

There are many ways to eat tomatoes but some of the most popular are raw, like in a salsa or salad, or cooked as a sauce for pizza or spaghetti.

Every year in a small Spanish town called Bunol, there is a festival called La Tomatina. As many as forty thousand people show up to throw one hundred and fifty thousand tomatoes at each other.

Now that's one big food fight!

How do you know
when an avocado turns bad?
When it becomes *guacamoldy*.

What did the guacamole teacher say
to the guacamole student when he
said a dog ate his homework?
You've *guac* to be kidding me.

What did dad say when
you ate the last of the dip and chips?
You've hit *quac* bottom.

Which vegetable goes
best with jacket potatoes?
Button mushrooms.

What kind of vegetables are sold at the zoo?
Zoo-chini.

Why did the cabbage win the race?
Because it was ahead.

What's a potato's favorite
form of transportation?
A gravy train.

How does a mushroom clean the house?

With a *mushbroom*.

What do you call a round, green vegetable that
breaks out of prison?
An *escapea*.

What's green and goes to summer camp?
Brussel scout.

What do you call a mischievous egg?
A practical *yolker*.

What has to be broken before you can use it?
An egg.

What do you call a city with 20 million eggs?
New *Yolk* City.

Where is the best place to learn about eggs?
The *Hencyclopedia*.

What do you call an egg
that goes on a safari?
An *eggs-plorer.*

Why can't you tease egg whites?
Because they can't take a *yolk.*

How do clowns like their eggs cooked?

Funny side-up.

What do comedians eat for breakfast?
Pun-cakes.

Why should we not tell pancake jokes?
They fall flat.

How do you make a waffle smile?
Butter him up.

When is eating like school?
When you have three or four courses.

What's the heaviest food in the world?
Won-ton soup.

Definition
What is a three-course dinner?

You've all heard of a three-course meal. Well, what does that really mean?

A course is a set of food served at the same time during a meal.

For instance, a dinner can start with soup, which would be the first course. It would be followed by the second course, which could be meat, starch, and vegetable. Lastly, the third course could be a variety of desserts.

Is dessert your favorite? **Of course!**

Why did the skeleton go to the barbeque?
To get another rib.

Did you hear about the cured ham?
I didn't know it was sick.

Do not use beef stew
as a password on the computer.
It's not *stroganoff.*

Why is ground beef so popular?

Because flying cows are hard to catch.

How did the hamburger propose to the fires?
With an onion ring.

What's a spider's favorite fast food?
French *Flies*.

What do you call it when you
play Tug-of-War with a pig?
Pulled pork.

Waiter, will my pizza be long?
No, it will be round.

Why did the Hawaiian pizza burn?
The oven should have been on *aloha* heat

What do you call vegan meat on a pizza?
A *pepperphony* pizza

How do you truly enjoy a hotdog?
With relish.

True or false
The word relish is an example
of a word with a double meaning.

True - Relish can be a delightful combination of chopped fruits and vegetables to be used with the meal. It can also mean to enjoy something very much, as in 'she relished the joke.'

Either way,
do you choose to relish your relish?

What did the nacho say to the taco?
I'm *nacho* friend.

What do people eat in the library?
Shush-kebabs.

True or False
There's a library of smells in France.

Absolutely true - The Osmotheque is a library of fragrances in Versailles, France.

It was founded in 1990 and has over 3200 different scents.

Four hundred of them are no longer made and the only way you can smell them is at the museum. It is a collection of perfume history!

Many manufacturers donated samples to protect their secret formulas.

Now, that makes a lot of sense!

What do you call 52 pieces of bread?
A deck of *carbs*.

What happened when
they found a thief in the bakery?
He was caught *bread*-handed.

What do bread kids say
during hide-and-seek?
***Bready* or not, here I come.**

What did the bread mommy say to
her son when he failed his test?
You can do *butter* than that.

What did the daddy bread say to his kids?
it's way past your *breadtime*.

What is the worst thing about bread jokes?
They tend to get stale.

When does bread rise?
When you *yeast* expect it.

True or false
Yeast is alive.

True, yeast is very much alive.

Yeast is a single-cell organism and a member of the fungus community.

Yeast reproduces in a process known as budding. This means it grows, and is alive.

Yeast is used in the baking of bread, as well as beverages like root beer and kombucha.

Yeast has been around for thousands of years. In fact, a group of scientists revived yeast from a 4500-year-old container and baked bread with it to study how ancient humans ate.

It was the yeast they could do.

What is a pretzel's favorite dance?
The twist.

Why didn't the expired dessert
get invited to the party?
It was off-*pudding*.

What is the best thing to put in a pie?
Your teeth.

What is an electrician's favorite
ice cream flavor?
Shockalot.

Why did the ice cream sundae
ask for an umbrella?

In case of sprinkles.

Where do you learn to make ice cream?
Sundae **school.**

Ice Cream eating tip
How to prevent brain freeze.

When the ice-cold cream comes in contact with the roof of your mouth, your nerves react to the temperature, and report a loss of heat. This causes a brain freeze headache.

Simply place your tongue against the roof of your mouth to warm it and that sharp sensation will go away.

Well, that must be the reason we scream for ice cream!

Why did the cookie cry?

Because its mother ad been *a wafer* too long.

Which dessert is perfect for eating in bed?

A sheet cake.

When do you know it
gets emotional at a wedding?

When the cake *tiers* up.

True or False
Tiered wedding cakes
originated in Ancient Rome.

False - Stacking cakes one on top of the other was a tradition that began in Medieval times.

Multiple layers were stacked in a tall tower and the bride and groom had to kiss over the top. If they managed without the cakes tumbling down, they were destined for a happy marriage.

In later part of 1700s, baker, William Rich made his own three-tiered wedding cake. He designed it to look like the steeple of St. McBride's church in London. It became a new trend and soon everybody was taking tier cakes to the highest level.

Now that takes the cake!

How do you make a walnut laugh?
Crack it up.

Why was the boy okay after
he got hit in the head by a can of soda?
It was a soft drink.

Think about this...

What has words but never speaks?

A book.

Animals
Down on the Farm

What do you call a goat that
likes martial arts?
The karate kid.

What does a bored goat say?
Meh.

What did the baby goats say to the farmer when
they pranked him?
Just kidding.

What did the pig say to the farmer?
You take me for *grunted*.

What do you call a pig that
got fired from his job?
Canned ham.

Why'd the pig take a bath.

Because the farmer said, "Hogwash."

Why did the lamb cross the road?

To get to the *baaaarber* shop.

What do you call 100 sheep
rolling down a hill?

A *lambslide.*

How many sheep does
it take to knit a sweater?
None. Sheep don't knit.

**Definition
Hogwash was a word first
created in the fifteenth century.**

Leftover liquids were mixed with garbage from the kitchen and fed to the pigs or hogs.

Today when someone says hogwash in a conversation, they are stating that an idea is silly or makes no sense.

**Sounds like a bunch of baloney to me!
(Baloney is another word for nonsense,
but that's a different story).**

Where do sheep take a bath?
In the *baaathtub*.

What do you call a sheep with no legs?
A cloud.

Where do sheep go to watch funny videos?
Ewe **tube.**

What do you call cattle with a sense of humor?
Laughing stock.

Why is it hard to have
a conversation with a bull?
They always *butt* in.

Why was the cow afraid?
He was a *cow-herd.*

Why did the cow cross the road?

Because the chicken was on vacation.

What do you call a cow that eats your grass?
A lawn *moo-er.*

What's a cow's favorite party game?
***Mooosical* chairs.**

True or False
Cows can't climb upstairs

True - Cows can walk downstairs but not upstairs. The shape of their knees are only good for descending steps.

If you walking down the steps behind them, you've got to remember say, *mooov- it!*

What does a French cow say?

Moo la la.

What do you call a girly cow?
Dairy queen.

What kind of money does a cow use?
Moola.

Why don't cows have a lot of money?
Because farmers have milked them dry.

What do you use to count a herd of cattle?
A *cowculator*.

What did the mommy cow say to the calf?
It's *pasture* bedtime.

How do horses stay in great shape?

They keep a stable diet.

What do you call a horse that lives next door?
A *neigh*-bor.

Where do horses go when they're sick?
To the *horsepital.*

What did the horse say when it fell?
I've fallen and I can't *giddy up.*

What did the man say when the horse walked into his store?
Why the long face?

True or false
Giddy-up is a command
to the horse to be happy.

False - Giddy up originated as get up when farmers or cowboys commanded their horses to begin walking.

Sometimes you just have to make the horse go faster, or you'll *stirrup* trouble!

What do chickens study in school?
Eggonomics.

What do you call a bird that's afraid to fly?
A chicken.

Why did the baby chick cross the road?
It was *take your child* to work day!

What do you call a chicken that will
only lay eggs in the winter?
A spring chicken.

What do you call a rooster that
wakes you up in the morning?
An alarm *cluck*.

What do roosters have in
common with baseball?
They both have *fowl* plays.

Why do ducks quack?
Because they can't oink, cluck, or moo.

True or false
A spring chicken is named
for its bouncy walk.

False - Spring chickens are young chickens, and when used for a person, it means that they appear to be very young.

That might be laying it on pretty *chick!*

What was the goal of the detective duck?
To *quack* the case.

Why do ducks fly south for the winter?
Because it's too far to waddle.

What happens when ducks like a joke?
They *quack* up.

What has fangs and webbed feet?

Count *Duckula*.

What did the duck say
when he dropped the dishes?
I hope I didn't *quack* any.

What did the duck say when buying lipstick?
Put it on my bill.

Where do you find a turkey with no legs?
Where you left it.

**True or false
Ducks have teeth.**

True - Well, sort of, true. Every species of ducks have different shaped bills, but they all have one thing in common, a serrated edge called lamellae.

Lamellae are thin, fringe-like shapes on the side of the bill.

These 'teeth' help keep the mud and water from the food they eat. The size and shape of a duck bill indicate its type of diet.

Long, flat bills mean the duck eats plants. Sharper bills enable the ducks to eat small fish.

**Whatever he's eating,
I'm sure he puts the charge on his bill!**

Cats, Dogs, and Mice

Why do you need a license
for a dog but not for a cat?

Cats can't drive.

Why does a dog wag its tail?
Because there's no one else to wag it for him

What do you do if your
dog chews a dictionary?

Take the words out of his mouth.

True or False
The first dictionary had 300,000 words.

False - One of the earliest dictionaries in the English language was called the "Table Alphabeticall." It was produced in 1604 by Robert Cawdrey, and contained approximately 3,000 words.

Now that's a lot of letters to deliver!

What do you call a cold dog
sitting on a bunny?

A *chili* dog on a bun.

Why did the dog cross the road twice?
He was trying to fetch a boomerang.

True or False
The boomerang is actually a weapon.

True - The boomerang originates from the native population of Australia. Made from bone or wood, it's a v-shaped carved tool, designed to return to the person who threw it after it's thrown.

They were originally used for hunting or fighting. They can be works of art and natives often painted pictures that represented their stories and traditions.

You might say it comes in handy.

What happens when it rains cats and dogs?
I don't know but you can step in a *poodle*.

What kind of kitten works for the Red Cross?

A first aid *kit*.

What kind of cat likes to live in water?
An *octo-puss*.

What has the fur of a cat, the whiskers of a cat, and the ears and tail of a cat, but is not a cat?
A kitten.

What's a cat's favorite dessert?
Chocolate *mouse.*

True or false
There was once a river
made from chocolate.

True - In 1971, when filming the movie Willy Wonka and the Chocolate Factory, the director had a chocolate river made with 15000 gallons of water, mixed with milk and cream.

The cream spoiled quickly and the cast and crew complained that the river smelled horrible.

I guess they should have used almost milk. It's not like any *udder* milk.

There were ten cats in a boat and one jumped out. How many were left?

None, they were all copycats.

Why was the cat afraid of a tree?

Because of the bark.

What do you call a cat wearing shoes?

Puss in boots.

What is a cat's favorite movie?

The Sound of *Mew-sic*.

How do two cats end a fight?
They hiss and make up.

What do you call a pile of cats?
A *meow-tain.*

How do cats stop crime?

***Claw* enforcement.**

Why do cats always get their way?
They're very *purr-suasive.*

Where do mice park their boats?
At the hickory dickery dock.

How do you get a mouse to smile?

Say *cheese!*

Why was the mouse afraid
to go into the water?
Catfish.

True or False
Catfish never stop growing.

True - Catfish grow continually.

The older a fish, the bigger it becomes.

On average, a catfish can weigh between 2 to 7 pounds. They measure between 12 to14 inches long.

There are catfish that have grown to a huge 58 pounds, measuring 52 inches in length!

It's been reported that a fisherman in Northern Thailand caught a huge fish in the Mekong River.

It was nearly nine feet long and weighed 646 pounds!

Now that's a lot of fish!

Jungle Animals

Why do lions eat raw meat?
Because they don't know how to cook.

How do lions like to pass the time?
They like lion around.

What do you call an
elephant in a phone booth?

Stuck.

How do lions like to pass the time?
They like *lion* around.

What game should you never
play with an elephant?
Squash.

How are elephants and trees alike?
They both have trunks.

What do you call an elephant
that doesn't matter?
An *irrelephant*.

Why did the elephant
paint his fingernails red?
So he could hide in a box of cherries.

What does Tarzan say when
he sees a herd of elephants?

"Look, a herd of elephants."

What is as big as an elephant
but weighs nothing?
His shadow.

When does a rhino go *moo*?

When he's learning a new language.

What's gray but turns red?

An embarrassed rhino.

What's a hyena's favorite cookie?

A snickerdoodle.

How do you get a hippopotamus
to do whatever you want?

Hipponotism.

How do you inoculate a hippo?
With a *hippodemic* needle.

True or False
Hippos live in packs.

False - Hippos live in herds of around ten to twenty individuals.

There is one dominant male who protects the others.

Female hippos are called cows and give birth every two years.

Do you know why you never see hippos hiding in trees?

'Cause they're really good at it!

What did the giraffe get bad grades?

He had his head in the clouds.

What do you call it when a giraffe
swallows a toy jet?
A *plane* in the neck.

What do you call it
when two giraffes collide?
A *giraffic* jam.

Why did the monkey go to law school?
He wanted to study the Law of the Jungle.

What do you call it
when a bunch of chimps starts a business?

Monkey business.

What did the monkey say
when he cut off his tail?
It won't be long now.

Why did the monkey like the banana?
Because it had *appeal*.

What's a monkey's favorite dance move?
A banana split.

How do monkeys get down the stairs?
They slide down the *banana-ster.*

What do you call an angry monkey?
***Furious* George.**

Why can't a leopard hide?
Because he's always spotted.

Which side of the leopard
has the most spots?
The outside.

What did the leopard say
after he ate his lunch?
That hit the spot.

What do you call a place
where an octopus is sitting?
Octopied.

What does an octopus
wear when it gets cold?

A coat of arms.

What did the sardine call the submarine?
A can of people.

What kind of dance was the frog best at?
Hip hop.

Why don't fish like basketball?
They're afraid of the nets.

What's the easiest way to catch a fish?
Have someone throw it to you.

How do you make goldfish old?
Take away the g.

What did the Cinderella
fish wear to the ball?
A glass *flipper*.

Where do orcas hear music?
Orca-stras.

What was King Arthur's favorite fish?
Swordfish.

Why did the swordfish
win the best-dressed award?
Because he always looks sharp.

What did the shark say
after he ate the clownfish.
"Gee, that tasted funny."

How do shellfish go to the hospital?

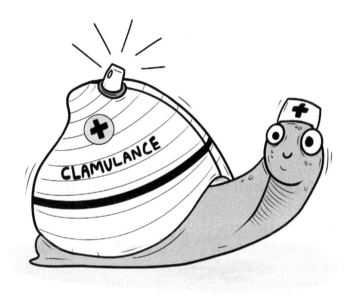

In a *clamulance*.

What is black and white, and red all over?
A sunburnt penguin.

Did you hear about the
romance in the fish tank?
It was a case of *guppy* love.

What do turtles, eggs,
and beaches all have in common?
Shells.

True or False
A seashell is just a decorative object.

False - The seashell is actually part of the animal's body. It's the protective outer layer.

When you find an empty shell on the beach it usually means the animal inside has died.

Seashells were used by Native Americans as money. Many ancient cultures used seashells as tools or utensils.

So, next time you're at the beach, seek and you *shell* find!

How does a penguin build his house?

Igloos it together.

What do you give a sick bird?
A tweetment.

Where do birds invest their money?
In the stork market.

What do you call birds that stick together?
Vel-crows

When does a teacher carry birdseed?
When there's a *parrot*-teacher conference.

What do you call two birds in love?
Tweethearts.

What kind of books do owls like?

Woot dun-its.

What do you call a magic owl?
Whooo-dini.

How do you stop getting
butterflies in your stomach?
Stop eating caterpillars.

Why did the moth nibble
a hole in the carpet?
She wanted to see a floor show.

What was the firefly's favorite dance?
The *glitterbug*.

What did the dragon say
after laying fifty eggs?
I'm *egg-shausted*.

Forest Critters

What do bees do when they need a ride?

They wait at the *buzz-stop.*

What kind of shoes do mice wear?
Squeakers.

What do bunnies like to do at the mall?
Shop 'til they *hop.*

Where do rabbits go after they get married?
On a *bunnymoon*.

What's a rabbit's favorite game?
Hop-scotch.

What do you call a flying skunk?

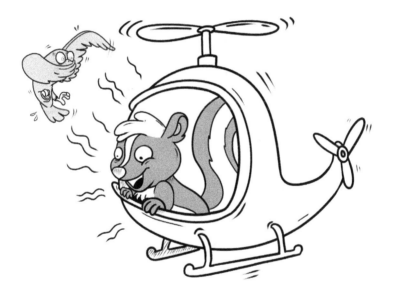

A *smelly-copter*.

Have you heard the latest skunk joke?
You don't want to; it really stinks.

How many skunks does it
take to make a big stink?
A *phew*.

Why can't you be friends with a chipmunk?
Because they drive everyone nuts.

Why was the chipmunk late for work?
Traffic was NUTS!

What kind of car does a raccoon drive?
A *furrari*.

Why is it a bad idea to work for squirrels?
They pay peanuts.

What do you call a raccoon
with a carrot in each ear?

Anything you want, he can't hear you.

What kind of nuts do rich squirrels eat?
Cash-ews.

What do squirrels do in the rain?
They get wet.

What channel do squirrels
like to watch on the tv?
Nut-flix.

Where do squirrels go for vacation?
Beech trees.

What do you call a sleeping wolf?
An unawarewolf.

Why did the panda get fired from his job?
He would only do the bear minimum.

What do you call an angry bear?
Nothing. You just run.

What do you call a bear that
doesn't want to grow up?
Peter *Panda.*

Why is a frog so happy?

They eat whatever bugs them.

How do frogs throw a tantrum?
They get hopping mad.

How does a frog feel when he breaks his leg?
Unhoppy.

How do you make a baby snake cry?

Take away its rattle.

Why are snakes hard to fool?
They don't have any legs to pull.

Dinosaurs

Why do museums have old dinosaur bones?
Because they can't afford new ones.

Why don't dinosaurs ever forget?
**Because they never knew
anything in the first place.**

What do you call a dinosaur
that has a fender bender?

A tyrannosaurus *wreck*.

How do you know if there
is a dinosaur in your refrigerator?
The door won't shut.

True or False
Stegosaurus was the
smartest of all the dinosaurs.

False - Stegosaurus actually had a brain the size of a walnut.

This four-ton dinosaur has a brain that was the same size of a golden retriever.

Its skull was so small, scientists once thought that its brain was located in its butt.

Do you know what the
stegosaurus did with its plates?
She served dinner on them.

What came after the dinosaur?
Her tail.

What do you call a dinosaur
who scores a touchdown?
A *dinoscore*.

What's the best way to talk to a raptor?
Long-distance.

What do you call a dinosaur
with a large vocabulary?
A *thesaurus*.

What do call twin dinosaurs?
A *pair-odactyls*.

Why did the dinosaur eat the factory?
Because she was a plant-eater.

Why don't you see a dinosaur on Easter?
Because they're *eggstinct*.

Think about this...

You are trapped in a room with three doors. Behind the first door is a pack of lions who haven't eaten for three years, behind the second door the only way out is over an electrified floor, and the third door is filled with poisonous gas.

Which door would you use to escape?

The first. *Lions who haven't eaten in three years would be dead.*

Let's Celebrate!

What do cheerleaders say on New Year?

Happy New *Cheer!*

What does a dog say on New Year?
Ruff.

Why is New Year's mathematical?
Times square.

What do you say to your
friends on New Year's Eve?
I haven't seen you since last year.

Why should you put your
new calendar in the freezer?
To start the New Year in a cool way.

What did the girl cat say to the
boy cat on Valentine's day?
You're *purr-fect* for me.

Why do we paint Easter eggs?
It's easier than wallpapering them.

What kind of jewelry do rabbits wear?
14 *carrot* gold.

What do you call a rabbit
that can tell a good joke?
A funny bunny.

How does the Easter bunny stay fit?

Egg-cersize.

What happened to the
Easter Bunny at school?

He was *eggspelled*.

Why didn't the Easter Egg cross the road?

He wasn't a chicken yet.

What do you call the
Easter bunny with a cold?

A runny bunny.

How does the Easter bunny travel?
By *hareplanes.*

What do you call a mummy
eating cookies in bed?
A crummy mummy.

What do you get when you drop a pumpkin?
Squash.

True or False
Pumpkins are vegetables.

False - Pumpkins are classified as a fruit, not as a vegetable.

In 2006, the pumpkin was made the state fruit of New Hampshire.

That will give you *pumpkin* to talk about!

What do female ghosts
use to do their makeup?
Vanishing cream.

Where do ghosts do their food shopping?
At the *ghostery* store.

Why is a ghost such a messy eater?
Because he's always *goblin*.

What tops off a ghost's ice cream sundae?
Whipped *scream*.

What do you call a dancing ghost?
Polka-haunt-us.

Why didn't the zombie go to school?
He felt rotten.

What does a vegan zombie like to eat?
Graaains.

What does a vampire fear most?

Tooth decay.

What is a vampire's favorite holiday?
Fangsgiving.

Do vampires bite family?
Only if they are blood brothers.

True or False
Bats attract insects.

False - Most bats eat insects.

This is important on farms where crops could be destroyed by insects.

Bats play a role in keeping us healthy.

Mosquitoes spread disease and bats keep their population under control.

A single bat is capable of eating up to 1,200 mosquitoes in an hour.

And everybody knows mosquitos can drive you batty!

Why did the vampire need mouthwash?
Because he had *bat* breath.

Why did the vampire go out?
For a bite.

Why can't you tell a skeleton a secret?
Because it goes in one ear and out the other.

What do skeletons say before eating?
Bone appetite.

How do you make a skeleton laugh?
You tickle his funny bone.

What did the skeleton
refuse to cross the road?
There was a dog on the other side.

What goes *Ha-ha-ha! Thud!*
And keeps laughing?
A monster laughing his head off.

What's a monster's favorite play?
Romeo and *Ghouliet.*

Why is tricking or treating
so hard with twin witches?
You don't know which witch is which.

Why don't mummies like to go on vacation?
They don't like to unwind.

Why did the cyclops give up teaching?
He only had one pupil.

Where do werewolves buy gifts?
***Beast* Buy.**

What do you call a running turkey?
Fast food.

Why did the turkey join the band?

So he could try out his drumsticks.

True or False
Ben Franklin wanted to make the wild turkey the United States national bird.

True - Ben Franklin wanted the turkey to be the United States national bird.

He said "a much more respectable Bird, and ... a true original Native of America..."

He was not too crazy about the other choice, the bald eagle, "... is a Bird of bad moral Character. He does not get his Living honestly..."

I guess Franklin thought one bird was *ill-eagle*, but his friends must have felt the turkey less *talon-ed*?.

What's the best way to stuff a turkey?

Serve him lots of pizza and ice cream.

What is the best dance on Thanksgiving?
The turkey trot.

What sound does a limping turkey make?
Wobble, wobble, wobble.

What did the turkey say to the computer?
Google, google, google.

How do abominable snowmen
greet each other?
***Ice* to see you.**

Why is Santa good at karate?

He wears a black belt.

What is a snowman's favorite game?
***Ice* spy with my little eye...**

What is a snowman's favorite breakfast?
Ice Crispy Treats.

True or False
"Silent Night" was first performed with a full orchestra.

False - The song "Silent Night," was first sung at a church service in Austria. The church organ was so rusted they had to use a guitar.

I guess they were lucky they found a guitar, otherwise it might have been a silent night!

What do you call people who are afraid of Santa Claus?

Claustrophobic.

Think about this...

What question can you ask all day long, get different answers each time and all the answers are always correct?

What time is it?

Funny you should ask...

What did the house wear?

Address.

What did the thumb say to the finger?

I'm in *glove* with you.

Did you know that people have worn gloves as far back as Ancient Greece, Rome, and Egypt?

Gloves were found in King Tut's tomb dating back from the 14th century B.C.

This might mean that the Egyptians may have had a hand in inventing gloves.

How do you make a band stand?

Take away their chairs.

Where is the best place to sit
when a submarine is diving?

Inside.

What did the clock do when it was hungry?

It went back four seconds.

What do you call a can opener
that doesn't work?

A *can't* opener.

Useful information - In January 1858, Ezra
J. Warner invented the first can opener in
the United States.

The can was actually invented almost 150
years before the opener.

**How do you think they opened
the cans for all those years?**

What did the bandleader call his two daughters?

***Anna* one, *Anna* two.**

What do you call a joke you tell in a shower?
A clean joke.

What do you call a farm
where they make bad jokes?
Corny.

What do you call an argument
between two electric companies?
A power struggle.

What do you call a Jedi with one arm?
***Hand* Solo.**

Want to hear a joke about paper?
It's *tearable*.

Where do roses sleep at night?

In flowerbeds.

What time of the year do people
get injured the most?
In the fall.

What kind of currency do aliens use?
Starbucks.

What is a princess's favorite time?
Knight-time.

What do you call a tiny mother?

A *mini-mum*.

Think about this....

Janey and Kevin are sitting in the family room one night.

Janey is watching the news and Kevin is reading.

All the power goes out. Janey can't watch tv, so she goes to bed.

Kevin stays up and reads even though he has no light. How is that possible?

Kevin is blind and reads by using his fingers. He read with Braille.

Where does a sink go dancing?

The *Dish-co*.

Why did the genie get mad?

Someone rubbed him the wrong way.

Why did the car get a flat tire?
Because there was a fork in the road.

What's a ball that you can't throw, shoot, eat,
spit, bounce, or catch?
An eyeball.

What does a biologist wear on a first date?
Designer *genes*.

What happens when winter arrives?
Autumn leaves.

How do you prevent a summer cold?
You catch it in the winter.

What is the best thing to have in the desert?
A *thirst* aid kit.

What did the explorer say when he found water
in three different places?
Well, well, well.

What do you call a snowman's dog?
A *slush* puppy.

What did the snowman say when the teacher
asked him a question?
I have *snow* idea.

What becomes smaller
when you turn it upside down?
The number 9.

Why do bees stay in the hive for the winter?

Swarm.

What do you call numbers
that won't stay in place?
Roamin' numerals.

What is a math teacher's favorite dessert?
Pi

What dessert do they put on a rocketship?
Spacetries.

How does a scientist freshen her breath?

Experi-mints.

Did you know that when most women weren't allowed to work outside the home,

Madame Marie Curie worked as a scientist and chemist to discover polonium and radium.

In 1903, she was the first woman to win a Nobel Prize in physics.

Curie won again in chemistry, becoming the first person to win twice!

She invented a mobile X-ray unit during World War I to help soldiers on the battlefield be treated quickly and save thousands of lives.

She sure helped cure what ailed them!

What do you call a man with a rubber toe?

Roberto

What kind of water can't freeze?
Hot water.

What do you call friends who love math?
Algebros

If athletes get athlete's feet,
what do astronauts get?
Missile-toe.

How did the man build up his flea collar
business?
From scratch.

Which state has the smallest soft drinks?
Mini-soda.

Think about this...
What has day in it, but isn't Sunday, Monday, Tuesday, Wednesday, Thursday, Friday, or Saturday?

Today.

Why is a computer so smart?
Because it listens to its motherboard.

What did the mommy spider
say to the baby spider?
You spend too much time on the web.

What did the panda give his mommy?
A bear hug.

What did the traffic light say to the car?
Don't look. I'm about to change now.

What did the dog mom say to her puppy?

**Don't fill up on homework,
we're eating dinner soon.**

What did the big bucket
say to the little bucket?
You're looking a little *pail*.

What did the magician
say to the fisherman?
Pick a *cod*, pick a *cod*.

What do you get if you stick
your car in the oven?
A hot rod.

What do you get when you cross
a piece of paper with scissors?
Confetti.

What is confetti?

Confetti is assorted strips of paper and other shiny material which are thrown in parades or celebrations.

In the 14th century on special occasions, spectators would toss small candies and grains at each other.

Cake baked with colorful sprinkles is called confetti cake!

That's a party on a plate!

What do you get when you cross
an airplane with a magician?
A flying *sorcerer.*

What do you get if you cross
a fishing rod with gym shorts?
Hook, line, and stinker.

What do you get when you
cross a hamburger with a computer?
A big mac.

What do you get when you
cross a skeleton with a genie?
A wishbone.

What do you get when
two skeletons dance in a cookie tin?
Noise.

What do you get when you cross
an apple with a Christmas tree?
Pineapple.

What do you call when a boy banana and a girl
banana break up?
A banana split.

What do you get if you kiss a bird?
A peck on the cheek.

What do you get if you
cross a chicken with a cow?
Roost-beef.

What do you get when you cross a chicken and a
chihuahua?
Pooched **eggs.**

What do you get if you cross a chicken with a
cement mixer?
A bricklayer.

What do you get if you
cross a parrot with a shark?
A bird that will talk your ear off.

What do you get if you
cross a parrot and a woodpecker?
A bird that speaks in morse code.

Think about this...

What call is for help, written all in capital
letters, is the same forward as it is backward?

SOS

True or False
SOS is morse code for Save Our Ship.

False - SOS is an internationally recognized signal for help. It doesn't stand for any words. The letters were chosen because they are the easiest to transmit. "S" is three dots, and "O" is three dashes. **Can you tap out SOS?**

What do you get when you cross
Godzilla with a parrot?

**I don't know, but if he asks for a
cracker you better give it to him.**

What do you get if you
cross an owl and an oyster?

An animal that gives you pearls of wisdom.

What do you get if
you cross a dog and an owl?

A gr-owl.

What do you get when you cross a mouse with a
squid?

An *eektopus*.

What do you
get when
you cross a cat
with a fish?
A catfish.

What do you get when
you cross a fly, a car, and a dog?
A flying carpet.

What do you get when
you cross a dog and a hammock?
A *rocker* spaniel.

What do you get when
you cross a dog with a vegetable?
Broc-collie.

What do you get if
you cross a dog and a fish?
A guppy puppy.

What do you get
when you cross Bambi with a ghost?
Bam-boo.

True or False
Guppies lay eggs.

False - Unlike other fish, guppies give birth to live baby fish that eat and swim from the minute they are born.

I guess *any-fin* is possible!

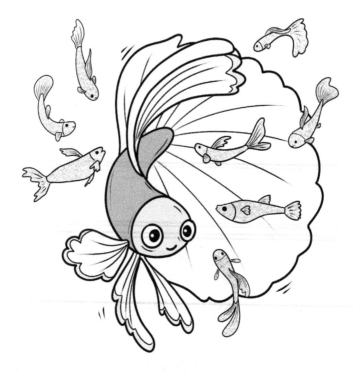

What do you get
when you cross a kangaroo with a snake?
A jump rope.

What do you get
when you cross a popsicle with a frog?
A *hopsicle*.

Why did the turtle cross the road?
To get to the shell station.

**True or False
Popsicles were invented
by an eleven-year-old boy.**

True - In 1903, eleven-year-old Frank Epperson mixed surgery soda powder with water and accidentally left it out overnight.

It was cold and the concoction froze.

He licked it off a wooden stirrer and named it an Epsicle.

He made more and began selling the refreshing treat to his neighbors.

Well, that's the scoop!

What do you get
when you cross a rabbit with an oyster?
The *Oyster* Bunny.

What do you get
when you cross a frog with a rabbit?
A bunny *ribbit*.

What do you get when you cross a porcupine
with a turtle?
A slowpoke.

What do you get when you
cross a turkey and an octopus?
**Enough drumsticks to make
everyone happy on Thanksgiving.**

True or False
Octopuses have blue blood.

True - Not only do they have blue blood, but they also have three hearts.

Octopuses protect themselves by shooting ink to hide from their predators.

They have no bones and can squeeze their big head and eight arms into very tight places.

I guess that's how they stay *octo-pied*.

What do you get if
you cross Frankenstein and a pig?
Frankenswine.

What do you get
when you cross a dino and a dog?
A *dogasaur.*

What do you get if
you cross a pig with a dinosaur?
Jurassic *Pork.*

What do you get if
you cross a dinosaur with fireworks?

Dinomight.

What do you get when
you cross a cow with a Smurf?

Blue cheese.

What do you get when
you cross a German Shepard and a giraffe?

A guard dog for the fifteenth floor.

What do you get
when you cross a giraffe with a pig?

Bacon and legs.

What do you get
when you cross an elephant with a hedgehog?
A twelve-foot toothbrush.

What do you get
when you cross a parrot and an elephant?
**An animal that tells
you everything it remembers.**

How do you catch a school of fish?
With a bookworm.

What do you call a snail on a ship?
A snailor.

Why did the cantaloupe
jump into the ocean?
He wanted to be a watermelon.

Why did the turtle cross the road?
To get to the shell station.

What do you get when you cross an elephant
and a witch?
**I don't know,
but she'll need a very large broom.**

What do you get if
you cross a kangaroo and an elephant?
Big holes all over Australia.

Now
you try it

Pick two very different subjects from these lists and see what happens when you put them together in a joke.

List 1	List 2
Cat	Blizzard
Cow	Parrot
Fish	Trampoline
Tiger	Ghost
Caterpillar	Drumsticks

See which response makes the funniest answer.

Milkshake

Frostbite

Fish Sticks

Walkie-Talkie

Scaredy Cat

That was easy- See what other great combinations you can think of to entertain your friends.

Use the next page to write out your answers.

Jokes can be powerful.

While they can be very funny and make us laugh, sometimes they can make people uncomfortable and hurt feelings.

Keep in mind that sometimes your jokes may come off the wrong way, so be mindful of what you are saying.

We also have to know when to stop. Keep it fun.

I hope you enjoyed this collection of jokes. Next comes an *Oh Susannah* story about what happens when a joke doesn't bring a smile to someone's face.

OH SUSANNAH - THAT WAS FUNNY, OR WAS IT?

Illustration by Mateya Arkova

CHAPTER 1

Susannah Maya Logan was excited to go to school. In fact, getting on the bus was her favorite part of the day. It was when she spent the most time with her best friend, Lola, and Lola's brother, Kai.

Susannah couldn't explain what exactly happened this past year. She began third grade a little annoyed with Kai. When she sat on the bench next to Lola during the ride to school, Kai had a habit of jumping up and trying to scare her.

The joke was on him, though. She and Lola got him back good last Halloween when they gave him a taste of his own medicine. They surprised him when he entered the playroom in Lola's spooky house, making him scream with fright.

Things had changed since then. Kai was acting much more friendly. When she went to Lola's house after school, he played video games with them.

At their winter holiday celebration, he gave Susannah a carved bird he made from a piece of hickory from his own backyard.

He painted it bright red, Susannah's favorite color. She placed it on her dresser and stared at it for a long time before she got up in the morning. It was a thoughtful gift, and Kai made it just for her. He gave Lola a matching blue bird. Susannah's mom, and Lola's mom thought it was sweet, too.

The bus gave a grinding sound and stopped in front of Susannah's driveway. Dad waved to Lola and Kai, who were visible through the window.

Lola was wearing a wool cap pulled down low over her brow. She looked unhappy. Kai waved back, but Lola watched them.

"Lola looks sad," Susannah observed.

"Hmmm. Maybe she's having a bad hair day," Dad replied.

Susannah giggled. They were always joking about bad hair days in the house, especially when they couldn't make Susannah's curls behave. It was even funnier when they said it about Mom or Dad if they were in a grumpy mood. It chased the doldrums away.

Somehow no one could stay mad once it was said.

"Don't forget where the Declaration of Independence was signed," Dad said to Susannah.

Susannah wrinkled her forehead. They had read about the Declaration of Independence last night after dinner. She couldn't remember discussing where it was signed. A bubble of panic welled in her chest. The test wasn't until Friday. She looked up to her father and said, "Where, where did they sign it, Dad?"

Dad tugged her braid. "At the bottom, silly."

Susannah let out a puff of air. "Daaaad," she groaned.

Dad was always saying things like that. He made her mood change, leaving them both chuckling. It started at dinner last night; Dad asked, "Why did Humpty Dumpty have a great fall?"

Susannah shrugged. She remembered the nursery rhyme but knew Dad had some twist on the words.

She wracked her brain for a punchline, thinking what might make sense but still be clever. "'Cause he cracked up?"

"Pretty good, but no. Give up?"

Mom placed the vegetables in the center of the table. Sometimes she attempted to give an answer, but not today. She changed the subject and asked about Susannah's spelling test.

"I want to know why Humpty Dumpty had a great fall!" Susannah's eyes were bright and merry.

"To make up for his terrible summer," Dad responded.

Susannah laughed so hard that she spit out her water. When it came out of her nose, both she and Dad couldn't stop giggling. Soon her stomach hurt, and Dad was wiping tears from his eyes. She had the same tears of laughter in her eyes. Mom held out a napkin to wipe Susannah's wet face. Mom was trying her best to look stern, but Susannah could see a very small grin.

Dad picked up a tiny cherry tomato from his salad and asked, "What did the mommy tomato say to the baby tomato?"

"I don't know," Susannah gasped between coughs.

"You better ketchup!" he shouted.

While she found that wildly funny, Mommy sighed, "Peter, that is awful."

"I don't think that's bad," Susannah said, squeezing a huge amount of ketchup on her plate. Mom took the container of ketchup away and put it in the middle of the table.

Mom said, "That's enough for you." She looked at Dad and said with a smile, "And you, too."

"Dad's just being funny. I like that."

"I understand, but we all have to know when it's enough ketchup and enough jokes."

Susannah thought about that. She didn't agree. Jokes made everything better.

The next morning, Susannah rushed past the first few rows on the bus and plopped down on the seat next to Lola. Lola's eyes were downcast. "What's the matter, Lola?"

"She's feeling low." Kai jumped up from the seat behind them and said it loudly enough for everyone to hear. "Get it, low... Lola."

A few of the kids snickered. "Maybe she's just having a bad hair day," Susannah said with a smile.

Lola opened her mouth, but nothing came out. Her eyes filled with tears. Susannah was sure she heard a sob and she realized these were not happy tears like Dad's last night. Lola pulled her hat down lower, turning her back on Susannah, and faced the window.

"What's the matter?" Susannah asked. She put her hand on Lola's back, but Lola shrugged it off.

Kai was cracking up. "Oh, that's hair-larious!"

Lola pushed out her lower lip and folded her arms over her chest. "I'm telling mom."

Susannah looked from Kai's face to Lola's. Lola wouldn't meet her eyes.

"See, she's really having a bad hair day," he said loudly. "Mom gave her a haircut, and Lola doesn't like the bangs." He tapped Lola on the shoulder and said, "You should have told her; bangs a lot. Mom!"

Susannah couldn't help the giggle that escaped. All the other kids were laughing except for Lola. A tear rolled down her cheek.

"Oh, come on, Lola. It's kind of funny," Susannah said.

"I'm glad you think so, " Lola said. "I don't."

They sat in silence until they pulled up to the school. Susannah started to say something, but Lola brushed right past her.

CHAPTER 2

In class, Susannah watched Lola pull off her hat, revealing a fringe of bangs.

"They're not so horrible," Susannah told her.

Lola took out her notebook, ignoring Susannah.

Mrs. Horn wrote a to-do list on the board, and they all took out their pencils to solve the math problems.

By lunchtime, Susannah was so upset that Lola wasn't speaking; she could barely eat. She pushed her half-eaten sandwich away. Lola sat next to her, her hand cupping her cheek, looking sad.

Susannah chewed on her apple, thinking of how her father would handle it. Joking about Lola's hair certainly didn't work, so she looked at her friend's sandwich and said, "What did the cheese say when it looked into the mirror?"

Lola shrugged as if she didn't care.

"Looking Gouda!" Susannah said with a smile.

Lola looked at her blankly. She went back to picking apart her bread.

"Don'tcha get it. Gouda."

"What's Gouda?" Lola didn't sound interested.

"It's a type of cheese. It's funny because I said, looking Gouda instead of looking good."

Lola shook her head. "I don't think it's funny."

Susannah thought for another minute She was going to have to pull in the good stuff. What had her father said that made her giggle last week? "I've got something funny to share. Two cookies were baking in the oven, and one said to the other, 'Whew, it's getting hot in here.' The other cookie screamed, 'Ahhh, a talking cookie!'"

Simon Samuels, who was listening intently, chortled and banged the table. Lola sighed, just like her mom did last night, and said, "Oh, Susannah." She sat up straight. Lola's eyes looked a little happier and she started humming the song, Oh Susannah.

Susannah hated that song.

Soon, Lola had a big smile on her face.

Susannah wasn't sure exactly what Lola found funny. It was just her name in a silly song. She really wished Lola would stop.

By the time they were back in class, Susannah's stomach was making a lot of funny noises. She squirmed on her seat, half-paying attention to the lesson. Mrs. Horn had each child stand and read one paragraph from the book they were studying.

As her turn neared, she was thinking of asking to leave the room for a break. The squeaks and squeals from her mid-section were louder and more annoying than ever. In fact, she was sure she heard Simon making the same noise from the corner of his mouth. He added groans, just low enough for the children in her immediate vicinity to hear.

Raising her hand to ask for a hall pass, Mrs. Horn nodded her head. Susannah rose to grab the wooden block they used as a hall pass when the most horrible thing in the world happened. The peeps and squeaks from the inside decided to announce themselves on the outside. Susannah squeezed her stomach muscles but only made the noise last longer... and louder. Susannah's face turned beet red. The class went absolutely silent.

Susannah froze, hoping to halt the noise, but it wouldn't have mattered. The class exploded with laughter. She looked at the sea of faces, all chuckling as if one little noise was the funniest thing in the world. Several people made the same sound; others pinched their noses and said *phew.*

Steven Mattsly put his hand under his shirt and imitated the noise with his armpit and his palm. Even Lola was smiling with all her teeth showing.

Mrs. Horn walked to the light switch and flicked them on and off, her signal for the kids to settle down. It had little effect. "Go on, Susannah," she said quietly, nodding to the bathroom down the hall.

Susannah ran to the restroom and never wanted to leave. She stayed as long as she could, staring at her pale reflection. Slapping a hand to her head, she wished she could disappear. The echoes of the laughter still rang in her ears. She shook her head. It wasn't funny. It wasn't.

Susannah returned to the classroom, her face flushed, and couldn't bring her eyes to meet any of her classmates. It didn't matter; nobody was looking at her anyway. The children were sitting quietly, their faces down as they read their assignments. She heard a snigger or two. Mrs. Horn tapped her ruler on the table, silencing the noise.

Susannah wished she could make herself as small as possible. Something poked her in the back. Simon touched her with the eraser end of his pencil. "What's invisible and smells like worms?" he whispered.

Susannah shook her head.

"Bird fart!"

Mrs. Horn looked up and put her finger over her tips. "Shush!"

Susannah slid into her seat, thinking that wasn't a funny joke at all.

CHAPTER 3

The ride home was no better. Anybody who dared to walk near her only did it to make the raspberry sound that imitated the noise in the classroom. While Lola trudged alongside her, she didn't say anything.

Kai caught up with them at the bus stop, his face serious.

"Lola, I need to ask you something."

Lola looked up. "Yes?"

He waited until enough people were around them and grinned, "Did you manage to test the big bang theory?"

Kai laughed at his joke. Lola compressed her lips and didn't answer. She stomped up the steps of the bus and slid into the corner of a seat. Susannah sat gingerly next to her.

As the children filed on, each one seemed to have the need to reenact the sound Susannah accidentally made in the classroom. With every hiss and pop, she slid lower into the seat. She wanted to ask Lola for the wool cap to pull over her head.

"Hey, Susannah, why do you have to watch out for ninja farts?" Simon yelled.

"They're silent but deadly," someone else answered. And so it went for the rest of the ride home, joke after joke about what happened to Susannah.

"It's not so funny, now," Lola muttered when they pulled up to her and Kai's stop. She squeezed past Susannah. Kai was ahead of her, waiting at the exit.

Simon took this as a chance to move forward. He made fart noises directly behind her seat to the delight of all the rest of the students. Susannah felt exposed as if she were alone in front of a hungry group of lions.

The noise was deafening on the bus. Susannah wiped a tear from her face. Kai and Lola paused at the front of the bus. They exchanged glances. Kai nodded to Lola. They turned in one movement and went back to sit on either side of Susannah.

Lola took Susannah's hand, and Kai squeezed himself onto the same bench. It felt good to have their bodies next to her, almost as if she had a fence around her.

"Farting's no big deal. Everyone does it," Kai said loudly, then he asked quietly. "You think your dad will drive us home?"

Susannah swallowed. Words clogged her throat. She didn't feel alone anymore.

Kai leaned over and whispered. "I'm sorry about this morning, Lola. I didn't mean anything. I thought it was fun."

Lola nodded. "Sometimes it is."

Susannah's voice was small. "I think, as long as you are laughing with someone and not at them, it might be okay."

They talked the rest of the way to Susannah's house, drowning out the students behind them.

Dad was surprised when all three kids descended from the bus. He called Lola's and Kai's dad to tell him, the children were together, and after a snack he would drive them home if that was okay. Their dad agreed.

The group sat around the table, not even an extra sandwich cookie lightening the mood.

"What happened?" Dad asked.

A big lump prevented Susannah from speaking.

Lola dunked her sandwich cookie and said, "The day started wrong. Mom cut my bangs, and I didn't like them."

Kai added. "I was joking too much about it."

"Let me guess; you went too far. But how does that involve Susannah? You didn't tease Lola, did you?" Dad was horrified.

Before Susannah could respond, Lola said, "I was being too sensitive. I realized something too. If I had a thicker skin, and not allowed it to bother me it would have stopped."

"No one likes to be made fun of," Susannah mumbled.

Lola looked at Susannah and said, "I learned there is a difference between joking around and being just plain mean."

"Who was mean to you?" Dad asked Lola.

"Not me," Lola said and looked at Susannah.

"I farted," Susannah said in a voice so low, that they all had to lean forward to hear her.

"In class," Kai stated.

"In front of everyone," Lola finished.

Dad sighed loudly. Susannah looked up at him. Please don't make a joke about this, her eyes pleaded.

Dad sat down on the chair next to her. "Everyone farts."

Susannah nodded. Dad continued, "Everyone, animals, babies, people. It's as natural as digesting food or breathing. We do all try to hold them in, but sometimes, the situation is impossible. The next time it happens, just say excuse me, and act like it's the most normal thing in the world. Their behavior reflects on them, not you." He hit the table with his hand, his voice loud and full of humor. "I ask if anyone here has never farted in public; let that person stand."

Susannah, Kai, Lola, and Dad all looked at each other, waiting to see who would be the one to stand. Dad half rose and groaned, "Oh, I forgot about that time at Aunt Bea's." He plopped down.

"Baseball practice for me. It was epic." Kai made it seem like he was bragging. "Although Lola's can be pretty ripe, too."

Lola nodded, leaned in, and whispered. "I got him in the car when we drove to Grandma's last week."

Susannah gave a watery giggle and smiled.

"You see, kiddo. A good friend will understand. Happens to the best of us."

"They all thought it was the funniest thing on earth," Susannah grumbled. "I learned that sometimes you can go too far, and it's hurtful."

"People get lost in the moment and don't realize the impact. It's like everything else," Dad said as he took the cookies off the table. "Everyone has to learn what their limit is."

"With both jokes and cookies," Susannah smiled.

Questions to think about?

1. What do you think is the purpose of a joke?

2. Why was Lola upset when Kai joked around about her hair?

3. What's the difference between the jokes during Susannah's dinner compared to the situation on the bus ride to school?

4. Why did Susannah's comment about a bad hair day hurt Lola's feelings?

5. How could both of them have handled that differently?

6. What happened to Susannah after lunch in the classroom and bus that made her feel differently about jokes?

7. What changed on the bus ride home?

8. What did the three children discuss with Susannah's dad?

9. How would you have handled the same situation if it happened to you?

10. What did you learn from the story?

AUTHORS NOTE.

Thanks for sharing your time with me. I hope you enjoyed the selection of jokes, as well as Susannah's experience with them. Remember, a joke is only funny when you are laughing with the person and not at them.

This book could not have been made without the assistance of the wonderful and talented people who helped put it together. Thanks to my editor and formatter Chrissy Hobbs at Indie Publishing and Leen Roslan for the delightful and funny illustrations.

Special thanks to Mateya Arkova for sharing her illustration of Susannah.

You can't write a book if you don't have the material. My family makes every day both fun-filled and joyful. Let's keep those giggles coming.

If you liked Susannah's story, check out *"Oh Susannah It's in the Bag"* and *"Oh Susannah Things that Go Bump,"* along with the rest of my series.

Hope your day was filled with laughter and you had as much fun reading my book as I did writing it!

ABOUT THE AUTHOR

Carole P. Roman is the award-winning author of over fifty children's books. Whether it's pirates, princesses, spies, or discovering the world around us, her books have enchanted educators, parents, and her diverse audience of children. She is one of the founders of the magazine, Indie Author's Monthly. She's been interviewed twice by Forbes Magazine. Carole has co-authored two self-help books. *Navigating Indieworld: A Beginners Guide to Self-Publishing and Marketing* with Julie A. Gerber, and *Marketing Indieworld* with both Julie A. Gerber and *Angela Hausman*. She published *Mindfulness for Kids* with J. Robin Albertson-Wren. *The Big Book of Silly Jokes for Kids: 800+ Jokes!* has reached the number one best-selling book on all of Amazon.

She writes adult fiction under the name Brit Lunden and is currently helping to create an anthology of the mythical town of Bulwark, Georgia with a group of indie authors. She lives on Long Island near her very funny children and grandchildren.

Her newest book *Grady Whill and the Templeton Codex* was released summer of 2022.

Her newest book *Grady Whill and the Templeton Codex* was released summer of 2022.

Turn the page for a preview.

CHAPTER 1

WHERE THERE'S A WHILL -

"THERE'S NO WAY I'm going to get in." I crumpled the pamphlet in my hand and tossed it toward the trash can. It bounced off Gerald Thurson's half-eaten bologna sandwich to land on the floor in a colorful puddle of orange juice. The paper soaked up the liquid, darkening, the vibrant pictures dulled as if it were being burned.

Someone pounded into my back, knocking me against the garbage can so that both of us fell over in a tangle of gangly limbs.

"Hey!" My forearm automatically shot backward, almost connecting with the soft cheek of Aarush Patel. "What the heck, Aarush?" We landed on the lunchroom floor. I raised my hand with a sticky wad of gum now attached to it.

Aarush was on his back, propped up by his bony elbows, his glasses lying crooked on his large nose. "Elwood pushed me."

Aarush rolled his eyes at the retreating back of the middle-school quarterback. "Ugh. This place. I wish I could get into—"

"Don't even say it." I stood, then reached down to haul him up. I brushed off the remnants of the bologna sandwich from Aarush's khaki pants. "You're going to have to be careful when you go past Ivan's house on your way home. You look like Processed Meat Man."

"Ivan's house?"

I gave him an arch look, one eyebrow almost reaching my hairline. It was a hidden talent, and I had spent hours perfecting it. It worked great when I needed to make a point. In this case it was about Ivan's pit bull, Marcie.

Aarush blew a gust of air from his mouth and with a nod confirmed, "Marcie."

He rubbed vainly at the glob of mayo on his knee. "Maybe the mayonnaise will disguise the meat odor." Aarush spoke mostly in a monotone. I don't think anyone had ever heard him raise his voice an octave much above a whisper. Right now, he was obsessing about the mayo stain. I knew it would bother him for the rest of the day to the point that he would miss the conversations going on around him.

Not that anybody is too eager to talk to him anyway. Aarush did just fine for most of elementary school until some aide let it slip that he was on the spectrum, then slowly kids drifted away. Playdates and parties became rare for him.

I guess parents thought it might be catching, like he'd cough and you could get infected with autism.

I'd known Aarush almost my whole life. He wasn't diagnosed until he was eight. The day after the doctors informed his parents, he still looked and acted the same to me.

"Leave it." I shook my head. He was smearing the stain down

his leg, his hands scrubbing and making it worse. He did that when he was upset. It was as if he didn't have a shutoff valve.

Sound receded and I knew he was attracting attention. Next would come the taunts. Onlookers made everything worse.

"We'll take the long way home, Aarush," I told him from the side of my mouth so no one would hear me. "Stop. It's okay."

With a sigh, Aarush picked off a piece of half-eaten meat glued to his plaid shirt.

"That's better than Potato Chip Man," I offered, trying my best to sidetrack him. Aarush was a hard person to distract.

Aarush's top lips tilted in what passed as an Aarush smile. I brushed off a cluster of chips onto the floor that was embedded in my shirt at the shoulder.

Aarush was the most serious kid I'd ever met, yet when he smiled, I have to tell you, his face transformed. It might have been slight, but it was there. His dark eyes lit up with merriment, as if he knew a joke and was sharing it with you. I couldn't understand why no one else could see it.

They called him Robot Boy or a lot of other less complimentary names. Aarush always took it in stride as if it didn't bother him. I always wondered though if deep down inside, it did. I know it bothered me. Over the years, more than one of my old friends melted away, as if I had to choose between him and them. For me, there was no contest. Anyone who'd make you pick one friend over another is not worth investing your time.

Not for nothing, he had been my best friend since pre-K, and he played a killer game of *Super Dude*, our favorite video game. Super Dude was the epitome of all superheroes, impervious to nuclear events, and managed to save the mythical folks of Silicon City without breaking a sweat. I don't like to admit it, but he had a few chinks in his armor, Master Disaster being his major Achilles heel. But what's a superhero without a nemesis? Pretty boring, I'd say.

I heard laughter, looked up to find the school jock, Elwood Bledsoe, and his group of followers, as they pushed past us kicking the garbage that had fallen from the trash can into the center of the room, turning the small pile of refuse into a more noticeable mess. If Master Disaster was Super Dude's enemy, Elwood Bledsoe was mine. You could say we had a history. My hands curled into fists, but I kept them hidden at my sides.

Elwood set his court up at the corner table. He was surrounded by the popular kids. He sat on the tabletop, breaking almost every lunchroom rule. The lunchroom aide, Mr. Mason, lounged behind him, his back to the wall, clearly ignoring Elwood's violation.

Mr. Mason was hired to watch us in the lunchroom and during recess. I was taller than him already and probably outweighed him by a few pounds. He wasn't a teacher, but some sort of all-around aide the school brought in to help with security, and other odd jobs needed throughout the day. Right now, he was manning the lunchroom making sure we didn't revolt from the crappy snack food they'd recently brought in. He had a poor excuse for a mustache that clung to his thin upper lip. His long hair was combed over his small head and tucked behind two of the biggest ears I'd ever seen outside of a circus tent. Those ears, I had learned, had very selective hearing. Mr. Mason rocked on his black sneakers, his beady eyes watching me.

"I'd like to—" I started. I was sick of Mr. Mason, Elwood Bledsoe, and school in general.

"Like to what?" Aarush interrupted me. "You can't win." He held up his hands, ticking off each point with his fingers. He could be analytical at the most inconvenient times. At least he had stopped fixating about the grease stain on his pants leg.

Only right now, I wanted nothing more than to retaliate against the bully. Adrenaline coursed through my body, but Aarush's voice persisted. "One, he's the school star, beloved by everyone. Two, he's massive. He could crush Super Dude with those ham-sized hands."

"He couldn't crush Super Dude," I said, horrified at the mere thought, interrupting him. I didn't care if I was rude. Aarush Patel was the nicest guy in the whole school, but that was sacrilege. "No way. Super Dude wouldn't even waste time on a creep like Elwood Bledsoe."

"Would too," Aarush shot back quickly, watching for my reaction. He was distracting me, just as I had done before to him, and we both knew it.

I shook my head. "I'm not doing this with you, Aarush."

"Won't matter. You will lose this argument." Aarush stopped speaking. He spied a wadded-up ball of paper on the floor. "What's this?" He reached down to grab it.

"Leave it." I kicked it under the table.

Aarush snatched it up. "That's the application. You were supposed to bring it home. Your uncle has to fill it out. I can't go there without you."

"Go without me? Aarush, wake up, bro. We are never getting into the Temple. No way, no how." Temple was Templeton Academy for those of us on a first-name basis with the best and newest school in the universe. Getting in was the dream of almost everyone I knew.

"Of course we are going to Templeton Acedemy." Aarush's voice was reasonable, as if being one of five hundred handpicked special students to attend the most exclusive high school in the world were possible.

"Besides"—I waved my hand—"my uncle can't afford—"

"Tuition is free," Aarush stated.

"And there's the extra supplies I would have to buy. I'll be going to Middlebury High with the rest of this riffraff." I gestured at the packed lunchroom. We still had a good part of the school year to go before graduation.

"There will be grants." Aarush was nothing if not insistent. He placed his books on the table and gave me his full attention. "I could ask my father." He smoothed out the application in the middle of the brochure.

"No. I'm not taking charity." Both of Aarush's parents were doctors. Money was never an issue. I was an orphan, living with my father's brother, who was barely old enough to take care of himself, never mind me.

I never revealed my past to just anyone. I hated pity. My parents died when I was an infant, leaving me to the care of my grandparents. Don't get all moony-eyed; it wasn't bad. You can't miss people you don't remember, and Grandpa and Mema were great grandparents—I mean, not great-grandparents; they were my grandparents. You get it, right? They were nice people. Sadly, illness took one, and the after-effects of a stroke took the other.

Uncle Leo, the son they had late in their lives, was now my guardian. While he hadn't seen thirty yet, he hadn't quite gotten the maturity memo. Sometimes he was overwhelmed with the idea of *me*. He was a shock jock at the local radio station and worked long hours. I think I got paid more than he did with the hour and a half I spent at the supermarket bagging groceries.

"Between friends is never charity." Aarush was organizing trash in size order that students had left on the table.

"Not going to happen." I shook my head, then looked at him. "It's enough, Aarush. The garbage is neat now. Throw it out."

I took an empty milk carton and tossed it toward the trash can. It bounced on the rim and, to the dismay of my audience, landed on the floor. There were a few jeers and some choice words, all relatively harmless.

A whistle blew. "Whill!" Mr. Mason, it seemed, had noticed my failed attempt at basketball. "That's littering. Pick it up." He stomped over, pointing to the crushed milk container, the whistle dangling from a chain around his neck. "In fact, make sure you two are back here at three. You can sweep the entire room."

"We didn't make the mess," I protested.

He came close to my face, his mustache quivering. "You threw the carton." He pointed to the milk container next to the trash that had fallen earlier. "So you made the mess."

"Oh, come on. It's just one container. We don't have to sweep the whole room," I complained as I reached down to toss it in the garbage can. "Besides, I have to go to work. I'll lose my job."

"Be here at three," he said through clenched teeth.

I could hear Elwood hooting a chant, his friends echoing him. "Clean it up! Clean it up! Clean it up!" The first bell rang, cutting off their cheer.

Mr. Mason smiled good-naturedly at them, sharing their fun at our expense and waved them out of the lunchroom.

I snatched the brochure off the table while Aarush cleared the rest of the junk. The paper was wet and cold, but it burned in my hand. I threw it toward the garbage without looking backward. I didn't see Aarush catch it in midair or see him stuff it in his book bag, nor would I expect him to intercept it. Aarush Patel couldn't catch a cold, much less a paper missile.

The second bell rang, letting us know we had to head toward science or suffer another disciplinary action.

HER SERIES INCLUDES:

Captain No Beard

If You Were Me and Lived in- Cultural

If You Were Me and Lived in- Historical

Bedtime Nursery series

Oh Susannah series- Early Reader and coloring book

Mindfulness for Kids
with co-author J. Robin Albertson-Wren

The Big Book of Silly Jokes for Kids; 800 plus Jokes! 1 and 2

Spies, Code Talkers, and Secret Agents
A World War 2 Book for Kids

Grady Whill and the Templeton Codex:
A Superhero High School Adventure